AF131417

BOOK ANALYSIS

By Tara Dorrell

Fight Club

by Chuck Palahniuk

CHUCK PALAHNIUK

AMERICAN NOVELIST AND JOURNALIST

- **Born in Pasco, Washington in 1962.**
- **Notable works:**
  - *Invisible Monsters* (1999), novel
  - *Stranger than Fiction: True Stories* (2004), non-fiction collection
  - *Adjustment Day* (2018), novel

Born in Washington, USA in 1962, Chuck Palahniuk attended the University of Oregon School of Journalism, from which he graduated in 1986. He wrote as a freelance journalist until 1988, but only began to focus on his career as an author in the 1990s. *Fight Club* was his break-through novel, written as an attempt to disturb his publisher, who had rejected his previous novel for being too disconcerting.

Since then he has seen five of his works adapted into films, and two into graphic novels. He is known for his interest in anti-consumerism, and often his protagonists are characters who have somehow been marginalised or oppressed by society, while his writing style is known for its use of temporal endings. He has won the Pacific Northwest Bookseller's Association Award for both *Fight Club* and his 2002 novel *Lullaby*. *Fight Club* also won the Oregon Book Award for Best Novel.

FIGHT CLUB

THE FIRST RULE ABOUT FIGHT CLUB IS YOU DON'T TALK ABOUT FIGHT CLUB

- **Genre:** novel
- **Reference edition:** Palahniuk, C. (2005) *Fight Club*. London: Penguin Random House.
- **1st edition:** 1996
- **Themes:** mortality, masculinity, rules and order, consumerism, isolation, social breakdown, violence

Fight Club follows an unnamed Narrator as his tedious lifestyle deteriorates, only to find a new sense of purpose with the fight club he and his friend Tyler create. The novel examines the destruction of a consumer-driven society and raises questions about politics, transgression and male identity. Although Palahniuk had never expected his book to be accepted by a publisher, it ended up winning two awards in 1997 and was adapted into a film starring Brad Pitt, Edward Norton and Helena Bonham Carter in 1999. It is often compared to Bret Easton Ellis' 1991 novel

American Psycho for its depiction of masculinity and material values, and has become a key part of pop culture today.

SUMMARY

BEGINNING AT THE END

Fight Club begins right in the middle of the action, with the narrator and a man called Tyler Durden inside a building that is about to explode. Tyler has a gun pressed to the inside of the narrator's mouth, and tells him that neither of them are going to get out of this alive.

From this scene, the Narrator rewinds, telling us in the first person how he had met Tyler Durden, and how the two of them had ended up in this situation. The Narrator had been an insomniac, when his doctor recommended that he go to "see real pain" (p. 19) by going to a support group. Taking his advice, the Narrator does exactly that, taking comfort in crying at the alleviation of others' suffering. It is at one of these groups that he first meets Marla Singer, another "faker" (p. 18), who just like our Narrator, is not really ill. The Narrator is irritated that she is intruding on his form of therapy, and the two agree to attend different support groups to avoid each other. The cause of the Narrator's insomnia appears to be his job and the constant travelling he is required to do for it. On one of these trips, he is lying on a nudist beach when he meets Tyler Durden. Later on, the Narrator returns home from his business trip only to find that his condominium has been blown up. He is later questioned by the police as a suspect for having blown it up himself. Needing a place to live, he calls Tyler and asks to stay with him. Tyler agrees, on one condition – that the Narrator punches him in the face. Although reluctant, the Narrator does, and the two realise that they love fighting because of how alive it makes them feel.

THE FIRST RULE OF FIGHT CLUB

The Narrator moves in with Tyler, who works both as a projectionist in a movie theatre and as a waiter at a fancy hotel. He also makes cheap soaps on the side, sold to expensive department stores. The two of them form a secret club that gives the book its name – Fight Club. The club is organised around a series of unbreakable rules, the first of which is the most infamous: "The first rule about fight club is you don't talk about fight club" (p. 47). More and more people begin to show up to the fight club, leaving behind the monotonous everyday world and becoming more and more in touch with their masculinity.

Tyler and Marla meet independently of the Narrator: one night Tyler rushes to the hotel where she lives, believing her to be suicidal. After this the pair begin an unsteady relationship, much to the irritation of the Narrator. He notes that he never sees Marla and Tyler at the same time, leading him to wonder if they are in fact the same person. Tyler shows the Narrator how he makes soap, before pouring lye on his hand and giving him a chemical burn. Marla and Tyler get into a fight after she discovers that he has been using the massive quantities of collagen taken from her mother's declining body to make fancy soaps. Following this, Marla calls the Narrator to examine her for breast cancer, and discovers that she does indeed have it. As a result, she returns to the support groups, this time as a legitimate member.

The fight club, meanwhile, has grown exponentially in size, extending across the entire country, and is used by Tyler to spread his anti-consumerist ideas. After the Narrator aggressively beats up one of the members, a young man he nicknames "Angel-face" (p. 123), Tyler decides the fight club is no longer as fulfilling as it once was. Thus "Project Mayhem" (p. 121) is formed, made up of the most dedicated members. As with fight club, the cult lives by a set of rules, and their aim is to bring down modern, consumer-driven society. The members are encouraged to leave behind both their identity and their happiness for the sake of the army being created. Questions cannot be asked, lies and excuses are banned and Tyler *has* to be trusted. Project Mayhem is just as violent as fight club, and attacks, bombings and vandalism are used to destroy society.

THE BIG REVEAL

One night the Narrator attempts to kill himself after being called from work by Tyler. As he is driven by a member of Project Mayhem he is questioned about his life, and becomes depressed with how insignificant it is. He is only prevented from steering the car into the oncoming traffic by his driver and interrogator. Project Mayhem continues, but Tyler appears to have vanished. The Narrator attempts to track him down, only to realise that he himself is Tyler, his suspicions confirmed when he calls Marla and she addresses him as "Tyler". "Tyler" then appears to him: as his alter ego, he is able to fulfil all the Narrator's repressed desires. On realising that he is the one creating explosives and leading Project Mayhem, the Narrator attempts to shut the project down, but discovers that not only has his boss from his office job been killed, but Tyler has prepared the members of Project Mayhem for his own attempt at destroying the project, and they threaten him with castration. The Narrator loses consciousness and eventually wakes up where we were introduced to him at the start of the novel, at the top of a skyscraper. Tyler plans for them both to die and become martyred as the building explodes. This is stopped, however, by the explosives failing to work and the appearance of Marla and her cancer support group, who only see the Narrator pointing a gun at himself. In what he claims is the only action truly his, the Narrator nevertheless shoots himself in the face.

The final chapter reveals that although his attempt at suicide injured him, he is alive and in hospital, visited on occasion by Marla. The members of Project Mayhem also stop by, continuing to address him as "Mr Durden" (p. 208) and informing him that they eagerly await the continuation of the project.

CHARACTER STUDY

THE NARRATOR

The Narrator acts as our guide throughout the novel, yet he is by no means a reliable one. Fed up with his monotonous life, he begins to attend cancer support groups to "see real pain" (p. 19), as when the Narrator assumes he is going to sleep, his alter ego, Tyler Durden, is actually taking over and running both the fight clubs and Project Mayhem all over the country. It is notable that we never learn the Narrator's true name – even at the support groups he always uses a fake one.

At one point the Narrator does notice how he never sees Tyler and Marla in the same room and considers the possibility that they are the same person. However, he fails to realise that while Marla and Tyler are not the same person, his own presence is almost entirely eclipsed in the face of Tyler's. When he is interviewed by a police officer for the destruction of his condominium, Tyler stands behind him whispering his answers in his ear – yet the police officer notices nothing. While

Tyler may not be more physically present then the Narrator here, it is his words that are giving him power and control over the situation. Tyler is the one really speaking to the police officer, with the Narrator as nothing more than his mouthpiece. Once the Narrator realises that Tyler is in fact himself, he becomes scared of everything Tyler has set in motion and attempts to put a stop to it. Despite his resolve, he is unable to do so because Tyler is always one step ahead of him – as they are the same person, Tyler knows exactly how the Narrator thinks.

It is uncertain who or what the Narrator is fighting against over the course of the novel – initially it appears to be the inescapable monotony of his life and office job, then the more general pressures of a consumer-driven world. By the end, however, Tyler has unquestionably become his enemy, as has Project Mayhem. They are a part of the Narrator too volatile to exist in the world, but while he may be the only thing holding Tyler back, Tyler is also a threat to him. At the end of the book it is unclear whether Tyler is still there in the aftermath of the Narrator's suicide attempt, or whether the Narrator has finally been left in control. Either way, the space monkeys who are a part of Project Mayhem still expect him to lead it.

TYLER DURDEN

Tyler Durden is the alter ego of the Narrator, although it is not until quite close to the end that this is blatantly revealed. Bold and charismatic, he is willing to do everything the Narrator wishes he could – have a relationship with Marla, create the explosives and lead a cult that is intended to bring down society as we know it. He works a variety of night jobs, as a projectionist in a cinema and a waiter, in addition to a soap-making business on the side. He takes joy in splicing nanoseconds of pornography into the films he works with and sabotaging the food he serves to high-end clients. Although he comes to the rescue of the Narrator, he also instigates the initial fight that leads to fight club itself.

As the Narrator's alter ego, he is always one step ahead of him, and knows exactly what he would say in an attempt to stop both "Tyler" and Project Mayhem. Throughout the novel we can see a variety of similarities between the Narrator and Tyler: both take an interest in meditation and Buddhism, as well as in explosives and how they can be used. The Narrator tells us from the start that he knows things "because Tyler knows this" (p. 12). It is only when it is revealed that they are in fact the same person that this begins to make sense.

MARLA SINGER

Marla Singer is the only major female character in the novel, but one who goes through significant changes. When we first meet her, she is foul-mouthed and vulgar, and the Narrator despises her for being a "faker" (p. 18) at the cancer support groups (which he also attends, despite not being sick). She enters a confusing relationship with Tyler, which the Narrator cannot comprehend, yet at the same time becomes close enough to the Narrator to ask him to check her for cancer. Of course, she knows nothing about his split personality, and as far as she is concerned has been dating the Narrator, aka Tyler, all along.

Being diagnosed with cancer softens Marla, and transforms her into a more traditional female character. She is the one who appears almost as a saviour to the Narrator at the end of the novel, when she attempts to stop him killing himself. Thus, she is no longer the brash character from the start, but the dream-girl whose purpose is to save the male protagonist. Yet even here she fails, as the Narrator does indeed shoot himself. Project Mayhem has taken on a life of its own, and as a result the norm within both novels and society of the woman whose only purpose is to aid the man to fulfil his destiny is thwarted by the cult that wants to overthrow all societal structure.

ROBERT "BIG BOB" PAULSEN

A minor character, the Narrator meets Big Bob, a former bodybuilder, at a support group for cancer patients at the start of the novel. It is only with him that the Narrator feels able to cry, although this is taken away when Marla begins to show up. Big Bob later reappears as a member of fight club, but his death is the catalyst that leads to the Narrator turning away from both Tyler and Project Mayhem, seeing how trivially they treat his death.

ANALYSIS

MASCULINITY

Almost all the characters in *Fight Club* are male, and the aggressive need to emphasise their masculinity is present throughout. Described as "a generation of men raised by women" (p. 50), it is clear that the members of the club feel disconnected from their masculinity, and the absence of father figures provides a reason for this. As a result, they feel the need to exaggerate their own masculinity, to counter the femininity they were surrounded by growing up. If their father figures were not absent, then they were in complete control of their children's lives. This still leads to the men wanting to increase their own masculine dominance, almost as a way of fighting back against the men who have pre-viously been the oppressors in their own lives. The members of fight club are men who seek to regain control of their lives via their masculinity. The book itself is incredibly male-orientated, with only two named female characters, Marla and Chloe. There is a distinct conflict between the masculinity and femininity that both Marla and the Narrator present, which adds another layer of anxiety for the Narrator. At the start he is obsessed with his Ikea furniture and attends supports groups just so he can feel something and cry; a fixation on furniture and heightened emotions are typically more associated with women, and yet here they are placed on the male Narrator. Marla, in comparison, is brusque and obscene, traits that are usually ascribed to men. As a result of fight club, however, the Narrator becomes more assertive and in control, which is particularly clear once we realise that he is Tyler, and has been in control all along. Marla, on the other hand, is softened by the realisation that she does have cancer, and is the one who begs the Narrator not to kill himself at the end of the novel, essentially taking on a clichéd but expected role of women in novels.

Tyler is the most vocal advocate for a more patriarchal society, and this is part of the reason that he creates Project Mayhem. For him it is a means to achieve the control that he feels society is lacking. However, while he is pushing for the men of fight club to assert their own control, he in turn becomes an almost God-like figure to them, and so takes on the role that he had tried so hard to exterminate. Yet even this is thrown into confusion by the Narrator's attempt to break away from Project Mayhem and fight club altogether, as it demonstrates how Tyler's words have become even more powerful than he is – while he may *be* Tyler, even he is not allowed to go against his own rules.

NARRATIVE POINT OF VIEW

The narrative point of view is a key component of *Fight Club*, which Palahniuk uses to both maintain and hint at the Narrator's alternate identity. Had the reader been provided with a third person viewpoint it would have been obvious from the start that the Narrator was in fact Tyler Durden. By using the first person, Palahniuk forces us to go on the same journey of self-discovery as the Narrator does. It is only once the truth has been revealed that we are able to look back and see how we were being given clues throughout. This is happening from the very start of the novel, where the Narrator states that he knows something because Tyler does. Later on, they both use precisely the same phrase – each crudely describing how he could "wipe my ass with the Mona Lisa" (p. 124) – even though one did not speak it to the other.

Despite this, there are instances where we are spoken to directly. By addressing us directly as "you" ("you wake up at Logan", p. 25), we are brought directly into the story, as if we are nothing more than another "space monkey" (p. 12). Even though this is a novel that is focused on the overthrow of mindless consumer-driven society, it becomes replaced with a different kind of mindlessness – and the first-person narrative forces us to become a part of this.

The Narrator himself is unquestionably unreliable: as the book progresses, the boundaries between him and Tyler become more and more unclear until their thoughts appear almost identical. The flow goes both ways too – as the Narrator's interest in living a calmer, more spiritual life increases, so too does the entry of religion and spirituality into the ideas Tyler spreads. Meanwhile, the Narrator's detailed knowledge of explosives and how to make them only exists because of Tyler's own expertise. It is because of this that he is able to know exactly why the bombs at the end of the novel do not go off, having been mixed with paraffin and so rendered useless.

LOCATION, LOCATION, LOCATION

In *Fight Club*, we are never given a distinct location where everything takes place: although we know that the clubs eventually start to appear across the country and that the Narrator finds them in Seattle and other places, the original could have been started anywhere in America. This allows the reader to identify with the men joining the club – it is available to anyone who feels like the underdog, and it presents possibility no matter where you are.

The few hotels used also hold some significance, most notably because of their names. While the name of The Regent Hotel that Marla stays at might denote royalty and luxury, it instead only emphasises her place at the bottom of society, a potentially suicidal drug addict, a victim of the world she lives in rather than the ruler of it. The Pressman Hotel where Tyler works is extremely prestigious and extravagant, which simply serves to highlight both his childish behaviour as a waiter, which he sees as rebelling against society, and the massive difference between those at the top and bottom of the social ladder.

There is also a notable difference in the house the narrator used to live in and the place he shares with Tyler. While the former was filled with Ikea furniture and was ordered, sterile and lifeless, the house Tyler rents is held together with "rusted nails" (p. 57), and is filled to the brim with stacks of magazines. The Narrator's previous home and lifestyle was literally blown apart, but this allowed him to start again, and take up a far more rough and ready – but authentic – life instead.

FURTHER REFLECTION

SOME QUESTIONS TO THINK ABOUT...

- Examine the ways Chuck Palahniuk hints at the Narrator's dual identity throughout the novel.
- How does the 1999 film of the same name compare to the book, and why do you think the ending was changed?
- Has Project Mayhem progressed to the point where it could exist even without Tyler Durden or the Narrator? Explain your answer.
- What is the Narrator struggling against in the novel, and how does it differ from Tyler's struggles?
- How does the opening chapter set us up for the rest of the novel?
- Why do you think so many readers found *Fight Club* such a relatable book?
- As the novel progresses, it becomes a battle between the Narrator and Tyler. Who do you think should remain at the end? Explain your answer.

- Examine the use of religion and spiritual ideas in the novel.
- Explore the ways in which *Fight Club* criticises the consumer-driven world.
- Why do the Narrator's feelings towards Marla change when he is initially so irritated by her?

We want to hear from you!
Leave a comment on your online library
and share your favourite books on social media!

FURTHER READING

REFERENCE EDITION

- Palahniuk, C. (2005) *Fight Club*. London: Penguin Random House.

REFERENCE STUDIES

- Godfree, T. (2010) A Generation of Men Raised by Women: Gender Constructs in 'Fight Club'. *Inquiries Journal*. [Online]. [Accessed 23 January 2019]. Available from: <http://www.inquiriesjournal.com/ articles/227/2/a-generation-of-men-raised-by-women-gender-constructs-in-fight-club>

- Jordison, S. (2016) First rule of Fight Club: no one talks about the quality of the writing. The *Guardian: Culture*. [Online]. [Accessed 23 January 2019]. Available from: <https://www.theguardian.com/ books/booksblog/2016/dec/20/first-rule-about-fight-club-no-one-talks-about-the-quality-of-the-writing>

ADAPTATIONS

- *Fight Club*. (1999) [Film]. David Fincher. Dir. US: 20th Century Fox.

www.brightsummaries.com

Ebook EAN: 9782808019644

Paperback EAN: 9782808019651

Legal Deposit: D/2019/12603/149

Cover: © Primento

Digital conception by Primento, the digital partner of publishers.